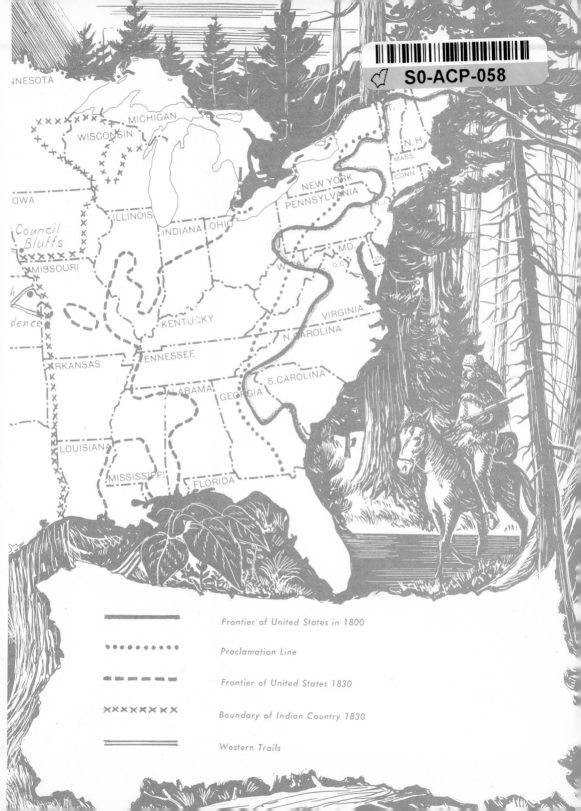

MINNESOTA

MICHIGAN

WISCONSIN

IOWA

ILLINOIS

INDIANA OHIO

Council Bluffs

MISSOURI

dence

KENTUCKY

ARKANSAS

TENNESSEE

ALABAMA GEORGIA

LOUISIANA

MISSISSIPPI

FLORIDA

NEW YORK

PENNSYLVANIA

N.H.
MASS.
CONN.
N.J.

MD.
D.C.
DE.
W.VA.

VIRGINIA

N.CAROLINA

S.CAROLINA

————————— Frontier of United States in 1800

••••••••• Proclamation Line

━ ━ ━ ━ ━ Frontier of United States 1830

×××××××× Boundary of Indian Country 1830

═══════ Western Trails

WESTWARD — With American Explorers

Here, in Walter Buehr's inimitable style, are graphic and fully illustrated accounts of the early adventurers who opened up the vast Americas during the years of great explorations. Included are accounts of Daniel Boone, Captain Robert Gray, the Lewis and Clark expedition, John Colter, Jedediah Smith, and Charles Frémont. Although the 1850's brought to a close the great American explorations, valuable discoveries by heroic men paved the way for other explorers and settlers. The West was open and what had once been undiscovered, wild country, was now land to be used in years to come for homes, farms, schools, and industry.

WESTWARD –
With American Explorers

Written and Illustrated by

Walter Buehr

G. P. Putnam's Sons   New York

Other Books by Walter Buehr

Through the Locks: Canals Today and Yesterday
Treasure: The Story of Money and Its Safeguarding
Harbors and Cargoes
Ships of the Great Lakes
Trucks and Trucking
Knights, Castles and Feudal Life
Railroads Today and Yesterday
Cargoes in the Sky
The Crusaders
Sending the Word: The Story of Communications
The Genie and the Word: Electricity and Communication
Keeping Time
The Story of the Wheel
The World of Marco Polo
The French Explorers in America
The Spanish Armada
The Spanish Conquistadores in North America
Chivalry and the Mailed Knight

Published simultaneously in the Dominion of Canada
by Longmans Canada Limited, Toronto

Library of Congress Catalog Card Number: 63-9691
MANUFACTURED IN THE UNITED STATES OF AMERICA
08212

Contents

WESTWARD –
With American Explorers

1. Looking West

THE year was 1646; only thirty-five years had gone by since that small band of brave men had landed on Roanoke Island to build the first English settlement in America. The few small villages and lonely farms clung to the coastline; behind them brooded the Unknown. Deep forest began just back of the stump-dotted fields where the colonists planted their meager crops. Hunters who had ventured into the forest after deer told of seeing range after range of forbidding mountains to the west.

In that year the Virginia House of Burgesses gave to Captain Abraham Wood all the land and houses of

9

a place called Fort Henry, about sixty miles up the James River from Chesapeake Bay, ten miles below the present site of Richmond, on condition that he keep a force of ten armed men stationed there for three years. Fort Henry was, in 1646, the westernmost outpost of Colonial America, and the starting point for expeditions into the wilderness.

In 1650 Captain Wood with three others made what may have been the first exploring trip in colonial America by Englishmen. They got only as far as the falls of the Roanoke, where they met unfriendly Indians, and so returned to Fort Henry.

Wood saw enough on this trip to realize that this was a rich land where fortunes could be made by fur trading with the redskins, and soon other men were exploring the wilderness. In the next twenty-five years John Lederer was first to climb the Blue Ridge Mountains, and Thomas Batts, Thomas Fallon, James Needham and Gabriel Arthur tramped through western Virginia, Carolina, Tennessee and Georgia. They crossed the Blue Ridge where they found streams flowing westward and believed that they must flow into the South Sea (the Pacific). Nobody in the world then knew or even imagined that the American continent was more than 3,000 long miles across.

In the southern Appalachians they entered the land of the Cherokees, a powerful tribe of fierce fighters. The first sight of a Cherokee village surprised them. It stood on a high bluff above the river, a village of large domed huts and storehouses filled with racks of dried fish and woven baskets of corn and beans, all surrounded on three sides by a high palisade of pointed logs. On the riverbank below lay a row of 150 large war canoes.

During the next seventy-five years more and more European immigrants trusted themselves and their goods to the hardships of a long sea voyage on the leaky little sailing vessels of the time. They landed at ports from Boston to Charleston and spread out into the backwoods behind the other settlements and farms. Everywhere they were stopped from going farther west by the rugged Appalachians which rose like a wall all the way from New England to Georgia.

Meanwhile the French were moving through the Great Lakes and down the Mississippi to the Gulf of Mexico, trying to encircle the narrow fringe of English colonies. The French encouraged their Indian allies to destroy any English settlers or trappers they found west of the Alleghenies, and so for a time the frontier remained where it was.

In 1673 the British government, partly to protect venturesome settlers and partly to keep the western lands in the king's hands, established a Proclamation Line. It ran roughly along the eastern slopes of the Appalachians from Quebec to Florida; no white men were allowed to settle or hunt west of this line. In a short time the pressure of land-hungry immigrants grew too great and soon pioneer wagon trains were struggling through the passes in the mountains and across the forbidden line.

By the beginning of the eighteenth century all the "usable" land in Virginia and the Carolinas was taken up, and the only hope of homesteads for the new immigrants lay to the west across the mountains in what is now Kentucky and Tennessee. The trouble was that more than a hundred miles of rough impassable mountains separated the older settlements from the rich new free lands. And — there were the Indians.

The Shawnees, the Cherokees, the Delawares and other tribes who lived to the north and south used Kentucky as a common hunting and battle ground. None of the tribes lived there, nor would they permit anyone, red or white, to settle. This was the "dark and bloody ground" which Daniel Boone, more than any other man, was to open up to the white settlers.

2. Daniel Boone

DANIEL BOONE was born in 1734 on the frontier of Pennsylvania. The sixth child of Squire and Sarah Boone, Dan grew up in the woods and often met the Indians who came to visit his grandfather's farm. When he was twelve his father gave him a rifle and he soon became a crack shot and a skillful woodsman. Within a year he was bringing in meat for the family table and selling deerskins and otter pelts.

When Dan was a tall, black-haired sixteen-year-old, his family moved west, marching through the Shenandoah Valley, the men with rifles primed and ready for

Indian or wild beast. They built their new cabins in the Yadkin Valley of North Carolina.

When Daniel was twenty-two he was hired as a teamster by the British army commanded by General

Braddock, which was sent to capture the French Fort Duquesne on the Ohio River, where Pittsburgh now stands. Everyone knows the tragic tale — of how Braddock refused to take the advice of a colonial colonel on his staff named George Washington, and so blundered into an ambush set by the French and Indians, where his troops were badly beaten. Young Boone escaped the slaughter by slashing the traces of his team and galloping bareback out of the ambush.

During the next three years a terrible war raged along the frontier between the French and their Indian allies and the British and colonists. Many pioneer families were scalped and their cabins burned; the rest fled back east.

However, by 1760 the French were defeated and lost their forts at Detroit and Pittsburgh and their control of the west. The land across the mountains was again open to the pioneers. When Dan returned from the war in 1756 he married seventeen-year-old Rebecca Bryan. In their long life together she gave him ten children and followed him from frontier cabin to frontier cabin until she died. For a while Dan became a packer, hunter and trapper. He was alone in the wilderness for months, and sometimes carved messages in the bark of trees for other trappers. One such tree which stood on the bank of Boone's Creek bore these words: *D. Boon cilled a BAR on this tree 1760.*

In 1765 he joined a party which explored through Carolina and Georgia and all the way to Pensacola and

St. Augustine, Florida. He liked Florida so much that he bought land there, but his wife always refused to go to live in the Far South.

Two years later Boone first entered his promised land, Kentucky. He crossed into Floyd County in the south, but found it too mountainous to take up land for farming, and so spent the winter there trapping. On May 1, 1769, he and three other men discovered the only good pass through the mountains at Cumberland Gap, where Virginia, Tennessee and Kentucky meet. Here they set up a camp and ranged the hills, trapping. While Boone and another man were out alone a party of Shawnee Indians captured them. The redskins were not at war, so they didn't kill their prisoners. They did take their furs and horses, leaving the two trappers their guns and just enough powder and ball to see them home.

Boone and his partner trailed the Indians, and when they made camp, stole back their horses. The Shawnees knew the country better than Boone and soon recaptured them, this time taking them along as prisoners. The two whites managed to escape into the vast canebrakes and lose their pursuers. After several days of hard going without food they managed to catch up with their friends, who had given them up for dead, and started home.

By now Daniel Boone had become a superb woodsman and a daring adventurer, who was always having hair-raising escapes from the redskins. One day while he stood at the edge of a steep cliff spying out the land he was cut off by a band of savages.

The redskins slowly closed in from three sides, so sure they had him trapped that they laughed and made fun of him. Suddenly Boone launched himself over the edge of the cliff and landed safely in the top of a bushy tree, sixty feet below. He dropped to the ground, looked up and gaily waved good-bye to the open-mouthed warriors.

In March 1771, after a successful winter of trapping he was on his way home with a load of furs rich enough to pay off his debts and buy supplies for his family. Again he was caught by Indians who robbed him of everything and left him to return home penniless and afoot.

In spite of the dangers, hardships and discouragements of wilderness life, Boone was still eager to move westward. In the spring of 1773 he organized a party of forty men, women and children, who started for the Cumberland Gap, their carts loaded with plows, axes, kettles and blankets, to carve out new homes in the forest. While they were encamped on the way Boone's son James, aged seventeen, and two other boys strayed from the trail and were set upon by a Shawnee war party who killed and scalped them. When they were found Boone sadly buried his son alongside the trail. He would still have continued, but the rest of the party had had enough, and so the expedition turned back.

It was lucky they did. For some time the Shawnees,

Delawares, Mingoes, Wyandottes and Cherokees had
been in an ugly mood. They felt they had been cheated
by the whites in land deals, some of their chiefs had
been murdered, and they wanted no settlers to drive
away the game in Kentucky, where they themselves
were forbidden by ancient custom to live. They roamed
through the forest, scalping lonely backwoods families
until life became so perilous that the pioneers aban-

doned their settlements and farms and moved back east.

Lord Dunmore, the governor of Virginia, decided to raise a body of troops and punish the Indians so severely that they would be glad to sign a peace treaty. The tribes were assembling, too, to sweep the whites back to the sea. Lord Dunmore was anxious for the safety of a number of surveying parties working in the "dark and bloody ground," and so he asked Boone to search them out, warn them and guide them to safety. All alone Boone made an 800-mile trip through wild, trackless country in 61 days, and got all but one of the men back safely.

The troops now advanced upon the Indian hunting grounds in two divisions, one under Lord Dunmore and the second under Colonel Lewis. While Lewis's men were encamped on the south bank of the Ohio, a war party of a thousand Shawnees under their war chief, Cornstalk, crossed the river and at dawn crept up to the whites' camp for a surprise attack. Luckily they were discovered in time, and Lewis's 1,100 frontiersmen, all crack shots, engaged in an all-day hotly fought battle with the savages. At dusk the redskins retreated across the river in defeat. Cut off from their families in their villages to the north by Lord Dunmore's division, they surrendered and agreed to give up all lands south of the Ohio River, and to let boats ply the river in peace.

With the Indians now quiet, the settlers began returning to Kentucky. In the spring of 1774 Boone blazed the famous Wilderness Trail down the east side of the Cumberland Mountains and then west through the Gap. Villages sprang up, among them Harrodsburg and Boonesboro, built by Boone's party. Now, perhaps, the settlers hoped, they could build homes and raise their families in peace.

It was not to be. The Revolutionary War broke out

and the British at Detroit armed the tribes and encouraged them to attack the American settlements, just as the French had fifteen years before. Again the pioneers had to desert their fields and cabins until only Harrodsburg and Boonesboro were still occupied. The savages prowled at the settlers' very cabin doors. One day Boone's daughter and two other girls were snatched by the redskins almost from the shadow of the palisades, but Boone and his men pursued so hotly that the prisoners were recovered unharmed.

During another attack on his settlement, Boone was shot in the ankle and would have been tomahawked had not Simon Kenton, another famous woodsman, killed the Indian and carried Boone to safety over his shoulder.

In spite of the Indian threat, the pioneers had to roam the forest to hunt. In February 1778, Boone was encamped at a salt spring, making salt by boiling away the water in a kettle. A sudden snow squall blinded him to the stealthy approach of a Shawnee war party which was on its way to attack Boonesboro. He was taken prisoner, but by a trick kept them from destroying the village. Boone was adopted by the chief of the war party, who named him "Big Turtle," and he was taken back to their village far to the west. Boone pretended to be happy in his new life so that his captors would relax their watchfulness.

Then he heard the Indians planning a new attack on Boonesboro, which he knew was unprepared. He had to warn his people at any cost, and at last managed to elude Black Fish, his new father. He ran 160 miles through the wilds in four days to give the alarm, with only one meal — some meat from a moose he managed to kill without a gun.

Luckily the Indians held a war dance and powwow, delaying the assault just long enough for the whites to strengthen their palisade. Then shrill war whoops issued from the dark forest, naked painted figures flitted from tree to tree and flights of arrows whistled over the log walls. The siege lasted for nine days, which was unusually long for Indians to carry on a battle, but the settlers finally drove them off.

The "dark and bloody ground" was still taking its toll of the Boone family in 1780. In that year Daniel's second son Israel and his brother Edward were killed

and scalped by redskins at Blue Licks. It must have seemed to the desperate frontier people that the savagery would never end.

At last Cornwallis surrendered to Washington and the war was over. The British surrendered the western forts, and stopped sending Indian war parties down on the settlements. The frontier knew peace.

Kentucky was admitted to the Union, courts were established and laws enforced. Then Boone found that, although he more than any other man had made it possible for the pioneers to settle in the state, his own land titles were not properly executed. He was told that he owned not a single foot of Kentucky land and that he would be dispossessed from his home. He had nothing to show for his years of sacrifice and hardship but debts.

Once again the Boones loaded their household goods on wagons and drove eastward into West Virginia, on the banks of the Kanawha, to make a new life. During the ten years he lived there, Daniel was a surveyor, storekeeper, guide and soldier. His friends and neighbors insisted that he be given a lieutenant colonel's commission, and they sent him to the Assembly at Richmond for several terms. Civilization couldn't hold him though; he wasn't comfortable in a land where the game had been hunted out. He said it was too crowded, he wanted more elbow room.

In 1799 Boone, now sixty-five, and his faithful Rebecca packed up again, loaded their goods on a couple of flatboats and floated down the Kanawha to the Ohio and from its mouth up the Mississippi to the mouth of the Missouri. He settled near there at Femme Osage Creek, on a grant of 840 acres given him by the Spanish government.

The Louisiana Purchase brought the Missouri country under the Stars and Stripes, and Boone was once again in trouble. His Spanish grant had not been ratified at New Orleans, and he once more lost his lands. Not until 1810, when he was seventy-six, were his titles restored to him by a special Act of Congress, because of his great services to the nation.

Boone was far from ready to retire. In 1814, when he

was eighty, he hunted and explored among the Rockies in the Yellowstone Basin, where his deadly rifle brought down buffalo, elk and grizzlies. At eighty-five he was eager to join an expedition heading overland for California, but his sons persuaded him to give it up. During his last years, after Rebecca died, he lived alone in a little cabin near his son's home, still broiling his venison steak on a ramrod over an open fire, and rolling up in a blanket to sleep on the floor, which he found more comfortable than a bed. He used to say he had never been lost in the woods, but he was "bewildered" once for three days. On September 26, 1820, Daniel Boone died, always to be remembered as one of the greatest explorers in America.

3. John Ledyard

WHILE Daniel Boone was blazing trails through the eastern mountains for the pioneers another American adventurer was discovering our Pacific coast, 3,000 miles to the west. He was John Ledyard, a Yankee adventurer, world traveler and explorer, who was born at Groton, Connecticut, in 1751. He went to sea early, joined the famous English explorer Captain

Cook, and became a Corporal of Marines on his voyage of discovery along the northwest Pacific coast. The ships anchored in Nootka Sound, Vancouver Island, in 1778, and here Ledyard saw great numbers of sea-otter furs which the Indians would trade for scraps of metal or cheap cloth.

Ledyard dreamed of the day when our Pacific and Atlantic coasts would be linked by river routes or roads, and Boston merchants could trade with Chinese merchants in Canton. When Ledyard returned to Boston he tried to get merchants to fit out ships for a Pacific coast venture, but nobody was interested. He went to Europe, where he met Thomas Jefferson, then Minister to France, and told him of his dream. Jefferson was interested but could find no money for Ledyard, so this intrepid man started back overland through Europe. Almost penniless, he managed to reach St. Petersburg, where he got permission to *walk* all the way across Russia. He got as far as Yakutsk in Siberia, but there Russian fur traders, fearing that he might cut into their American fur trade, had him deported. He died two years later in Cairo.

Although Ledyard died unsuccessful, his book and the reports written by Captain Cook about the rich northwest coast finally stirred the Boston merchants to belated action, after the British and Russians were already on the scene. They sent out two ships, the sloop *Lady Washington* and the ship *Columbia Rediviuus,* the latter under command of Captain Robert Gray.

4. Captain Robert Gray

THE *Columbia* sailed around Cape Horn and arrived at Nootka Sound to find the British and Russians disputing ownership of the sound. He stayed out of the quarrel and cruised along the coast, picking up

28

a cargo of sea-otter pelts from the Indians, trading one iron chisel for one prime fur. Then he sailed to China where he traded the furs for a cargo of fine tea, and returned to Boston by way of the Cape of Good Hope. He was the first American sea captain to sail around the world.

In 1791 Captain Gray returned to the Pacific and cruised up the coast as far as southern Alaska. He built a small ship, the *Adventure*, which could get into shallow harbors and used her to continue trading with the Indians. One day, while cruising to the south of Nootka the lookout reported great surf breaking over a bar. Captain Gray stood in closer and discovered behind the bar, almost hidden by fog and mist, the mouth of a great river, which he named the Columbia. A channel was found over the bar and the ship anchored in the river. The Clatsop Indians who lived along the shore told him that this river flowed out of the great Rock mountains far to the east. Captain Gray was the first white man to enter the Columbia, so it became a United States possession, fourteen years before Lewis and Clark crossed the Rockies and discovered its upper reaches.

Thomas Jefferson, now back in Washington, saw Captain Gray's account of the great river and remembered John Ledyard's dream. When he became President in 1800 he was determined that the Pacific coast should become American and that a good route across the continent be found.

At the beginning of the nineteenth century, as you will see by the map on the end papers, the population of the young United States was still crowded within the thirteen original states, squeezed between the coast and the Alleghenies. In 1800 there were only a few settlements and lonely farm clearings in that vast empty land between the mountains and the Mississippi which would one day be Ohio, Illinois, Kentucky,

Tennessee, Indiana and Michigan. The Mississippi, from the Great Lakes on the north to Louisiana and the Gulf to the south, was the American frontier.

In 1800 Spain still claimed all the land between the Mississippi and the Pacific coast from Canada to Mexico. From a fort at St. Louis on the Mississippi a Spanish governor ruled this territory, which was known as Louisiana. New Orleans, near the mouth of the great river, had been in Spanish hands for many years, and sometimes they closed the port to the American flatboat men who floated down the Ohio and Mississippi bringing cargoes of pork, corn and whiskey to sell or trade. It was the only outlet for the products of the American settlers living west of the Alleghenies, because there were no good roads across the mountains to the east.

President Jefferson knew that any foreign nation controlling the Mississippi could choke off trade at any time. As long as the easygoing Spanish held it there was not much to fear, but now ominous news reached Washington, the new capital — the Spanish had ceded Louisiana to France. Who knew what Napoleon, the power-hungry French emperor, might have in mind for this enormous new territory?

Jefferson sent James Monroe to Paris to offer to buy New Orleans. He arrived just as Napoleon had lost the island of Santo Domingo in the West Indies in a revolt, and was preparing to go to war with England. Luckily for the United States, Napoleon, deep in other troubles,

31

was willing to sell the entire territory, and so on May 2, 1803, it became a part of the United States, increasing the size of the nation by 140 percent.

In 1803 most of Louisiana Territory had never been seen by a white man. A few trappers had paddled up the Mississippi and the Missouri for short distances to find beaver skins, and many years before, French *voyageurs* had come down from Canada. There were a few small Spanish military posts in Arizona, New Mexico, Texas and Arkansas, and along the coast of California.

Nobody knew what lay in the interior of Louisiana. There were rumors heard from Indians of great rivers which flowed out of a lofty, snow-capped mountain range far to the west. There were stories of forests of enormous trees and of limitless prairies across which uncounted herds of buffalo thundered, of streams swarming with beaver. Captain Gray had seen a great river, the Columbia, which was said to flow out of those legendary mountains, the Rockies. Jefferson felt that if the headwaters of the west-flowing Columbia and the east-flowing Missouri were not too far apart, a water route with only one portage might be found from the Mississippi to the Pacific.

In 1800 fur trapping was a rich industry, especially beaver pelts. Every man in Europe who could afford it wore a tall beaver-fur hat, and fur-lined and fur-trimmed garments were in fashion. Jefferson thought that a good water route would encourage fur trapping and might even persuade the trappers in the rich beaver country in Canada to send their pelts down the Missouri to American ports instead of by the long haul to Montreal.

The President was determined to find out what lay in the new territory, and he had picked the man to lead an exploring party. He chose Captain Meriwether Lewis of the 1st Infantry, who was appointed his private secretary for a time so that he could learn the President's plans. He arranged for Lewis to take quick courses in celestial navigation, botany, geology, and zoology to prepare him for his task, then started him on his remarkable expedition.

5. The Lewis and Clark Expedition

IT was decided to send two leaders, in case of accident, and so William Clark, younger brother of George Rogers Clark, the famous soldier and Indian fighter, was chosen as co-captain. Lewis, who was twenty-nine years old, had once served as an ensign in a rifle company commanded by Clark, now aged thirty-three. Lewis held a captain's commission, but Congress for some reason made Clark only a second lieutenant. Nevertheless, Lewis insisted that they should always be equal in command, and so they were throughout the entire expedition.

Clark rode out of Washington late in the fall of 1803, arriving several weeks later in Pittsburgh, where he had a keelboat built to carry his men and supplies down the Ohio to St. Louis. At Louisville, Clark joined the expedition and they arrived at St. Louis in December, 1803.

The Spanish commander at St. Louis had not yet heard about the transfer of Louisiana to the French and of its sale to the United States, so he refused to let the expedition enter Spanish territory. Lewis and Clark had to make a winter camp at the mouth of the Wood River, a few miles upriver on the American east bank. In the party were nine young men from Kentucky, fourteen U. S. privates who had volunteered, two French boatmen, one interpreter and hunter, and a black slave named York, owned by Clark. There were also an army corporal and six men, and nine boatmen who were to go along only as far as the Mandan Indian villages up the Missouri.

During the winter they built their little "navy," which had to be very shallow draft so that the boats could pass over the many sandbars ahead. The largest was a keelboat, 55 feet long, with a 3-foot draft, fitted with one square sail and 22 oars. She was decked over at bow and stern to make a forecastle and after cabin below, while her waist had rows of lockers at the sides which could be raised to make breastworks in case of attack. There were also two pirogues, each with six oars.

Now came the endless job of filling the lists of supplies. They expected to live, mostly, off the game they killed. This meant they had to have ammunition enough to last them at least two years. Keeping powder dry and unspoiled when it had to be carried in canoes which might overturn in rapids, or on the pack-saddle of a horse which might tumble off a cliff was a problem Captain Lewis solved brilliantly. He had a number of small kegs made of lead, which, when filled with powder, were sealed so that they could lie completely underwater without leaking. When the powder was emptied from a keg and transferred to the men's powder horns, the keg was melted up and the lead molded into bullets.

The expedition was armed with flintlock rifles and several swivel guns, small cannon mounted in the bows of the boats. A good supply of extra gunlocks, flints and other parts was carried, and John Shields, the gunsmith, kept their firearms always in good condition. They also carried compasses, sextants and chronometers so that they could take sun and star sights for map making. At the last moment they discovered they had forgotten a barometer and a thermometer, and none was to be found in St. Louis. Their problem was solved by a resourceful doctor friend who made the instruments by scratching the quicksilver from the back of his wife's cherished French mirror, much to her dismay.

Supplies included a medicine chest, flour, bacon, beans, sugar, salt and whiskey, as well as many bales of trade goods for the Indians. There were shirts, coats, hats, handkerchiefs, knives, hatchets, awls, beads of many colors, twists of tobacco, and a supply of large and small medals with the likenesses of President Jefferson and of General Washington as good-will gifts to the Indian chiefs. The goods were to trade with the redskins for horses, furs or food.

In March, 1804, the Spanish commander at last got the news that Louisiana had been ceded to the French. He hauled down his flag and the French tricolor was raised, but the French had learned of the sale of the territory to the United States, so they lowered their flag at once and the Stars and Stripes floated from the staff at last. During that one day, Louisiana was under three flags!

Now the Lewis and Clark expedition was free to start. On May 14th, lines were cast off and the boats headed up the Missouri on the 3,000-mile adventure.

After several days they passed the last scattered houses of the French trappers and plunged into the unknown. Day by day the hunters brought in quantities of deer, bear and elk, as well as ducks, geese and pigeons. One day they shot five fat beaver, and also discovered two animals strange to them — a badger and a colony of prairie dogs, which they called barking squirrels. Everybody ate so lavishly that Captain Clark complained of the enormous quantities of meat the men ate and wasted. Surplus meat was jerked, cut into thin strips and cured in the sun to keep it from spoiling.

The party suffered a good deal from mosquitoes and ticks, and several men were bitten by poisonous snakes. They were beset by violent thunderstorms which often caved in the banks and changed the channels. One such storm drove the keelboat out of control and would have dashed it to pieces against a bar, had not all the men leaped overboard in chest-deep water and by main strength kept her from striking.

They discovered many deserted Indian villages, which puzzled them until they met one Indian who explained that all his tribe were off to the westward hunting buffalo. One of the soldiers, Reed, deserted. He was pursued and captured and made to run the gauntlet three times. This was an Indian custom, in which the prisoner was forced to run between two lines of men who whipped his bare back with switches. The strict military discipline during the whole of the expedition kept the party going during hardships and danger, and often saved their lives.

Now they entered the territory of the Teton Sioux,

a fierce, warlike tribe of river pirates, who often robbed the French fur trappers who passed their hunting grounds. They soon met with a band of these Tetons, who demanded presents and refused to let the explorers pass. The young warriors strung their bows, a warlike gesture, but the two captains refused to be bluffed. The white men cocked their rifles and prepared to fight. The Indians saw that although they could overwhelm the expedition with their great numbers, the guns would certainly kill many of the attackers. The redskins backed down, and from then on there was no more trouble from the Sioux.

The two captains usually got on well with the Indians they did meet. When they met a new tribe they would present medals to the chiefs and distribute beads, knives, handkerchiefs and other trinkets to the braves and squaws. They would tell the chiefs of the Great White Father (the President) in Washington, who wanted them to be friends both with the whites and with other tribes. They promised that when they returned from their journey traders would come to them, bringing guns and powder, blankets, kettles and hatchets to trade for their beaver skins. Most of the tribes accepted the captains' offers and supplied them with guides, food, and horses.

Early in November the party arrived at the mouth of the Knife River and the villages of the Mandans, a tribe which traded furs to the whites. The Mandans lived in large lodges half sunk into the ground, built on timber frames and covered with earth. Each lodge held several families, together with their best horses and large stocks of jerked meat, roots and berries. The villages were surrounded by log stockades for safety against the Sioux. The Mandans were friendly, and so, since winter would soon ice over the river, Lewis and Clark built Fort Mandan about a mile up the river from the Indian town. The fort was made of cottonwood logs

in the shape of a V, with four rooms about 14 feet square in each wing, and with a palisade across the opening. Here the travelers remained until the ice melted in the spring.

Among the party was a half-breed woodsman named Charbonneau, hired because he could speak the language of the upriver tribes. He was married to a sixteen-year-old squaw named Sacagawea, who had been captured from her tribe of Snake Indians living near the Rocky Mountains. She had a baby at Fort Mandan, and was, with her child, the only woman to accompany the expedition to the Pacific and back. Sacagawea proved to be very useful as an interpreter when the expedition reached the mountains.

When Lewis and Clark were ready to continue, the big barge was sent back downriver to St. Louis with some of the men. The main party left on April 7, 1805, in two pirogues and six small dugout canoes they had hacked out of logs during the winter. Lewis and Clark now had twenty-seven men, besides Drewyer the chief hunter, Charbonneau, his wife and baby, and a Mandan guide. On the 25th of April they reached the mouth of the Yellowstone River, and the habitat of the grizzly bear. They had never seen one, and were astounded at the ferocity, toughness and great size of these animals. They found that a grizzly with four or five mortal gunshot wounds could still chase and attack a hunter — only a shot through the head was a sure stopper. On May 5th they killed a giant grizzly which weighed at least 600 pounds, and measured 8 feet 7½ inches from nose to hind foot.

The country they were now passing through was well wooded, with many clear streams, and teeming with all kinds of game. Great herds of buffalo, antelope and elk grazed in the meadows, shadowed by packs of fierce gray wolves waiting to pick off a young or weak animal. Now they began seeing sheep with enormous circular horns; they were bighorn or Rocky Mountain sheep. The streams were choked by innumerable beaver dams and the valleys swarmed with porcupines, black and grizzly bears, while lakes held great flocks of geese, ducks and wild swans.

One night a huge bull buffalo swam across the river and stepped into one of the pirogues drawn up on the bank. Then he blundered through the camp almost treading on the sleeping men. In the uproar and confusion the buffalo escaped into the woods after trampling and damaging several guns, but no one was injured.

Farther along they passed a huge mound of dead and decaying buffalo piled up at the foot of a steep cliff. They learned that this was the result of one way the Indians had of hunting them. When they found a herd grazing near the top of a steep cliff, one Indian, wearing the head and hide of a buffalo, would sneak into the herd. Then a line of yelling braves would advance toward them. The decoy Indian would head toward the cliff followed by the stupid beasts. Just at the edge the redskin would leap under a ledge he had picked out, while the thundering herd, unable to stop, plunged over the precipice to destruction. Then the Indians skinned and butchered as many buffalo as they needed.

Slowly the boats moved upriver against the swift current. The men were often up to their armpits in water, doggedly tugging at the towropes. Their shoulders were raw from the ropes and their feet sore and bleeding from the sharp rocks. Many suffered from cuts, boils and stomach pains, but they struggled on.

On June 13th they reached the great falls of the Missouri, where they rested while Captain Lewis went alone to reconnoiter the way ahead. It turned out to be an exciting day for the captain. He shot a buffalo for meat for the expedition, but before he could load his gun an enormous grizzly lunged toward him. Lewis

started to run, but the bear was gaining on him fast, so he leaped into the river and prepared to defend himself with the espatoon, a short spear, he carried. Luckily the grizzly stopped at the water's edge and finally disappeared into the brush.

Lewis came ashore and hastily loaded his gun just

in time to face a snarling mountain lion, crouched to spring. A snap shot wounded it and it retreated into its lair. Later, as Lewis headed back to camp, three buffalo left a grazing herd he was passing and came charging toward him. He cocked his rifle and prepared to sell his life dearly, but the great shaggy beasts halted a few feet from him, pawed the ground and snorted, them meekly turned and trotted away.

Lewis found that the river came plunging down in a series of roaring falls and boiling cataracts for a distance of eighteen and a half miles. The canoes would have to be portaged around it, but the distance was too great to carry them. A tree with a thick trunk was found and the men sawed out a set of wooden wheels from it. They made a frame and axles and built a carriage on which they could trundle each canoe and their

baggage. It took from June 25th to July 15th to drag the boats and their loads up the steep ravines, around huge rocks and fallen trees to the quiet waters above the falls.

Their remaining pirogue was too big to portage, so it was hidden in the underbrush to be picked up on the way back. Lewis had designed a collapsible boat with an iron frame covered with skins, but when they tried it above the falls it leaked so badly they had to leave it too.

The country here swarmed with game. They saw a herd of 10,000 buffalo, vast numbers of antelopes and hundreds of grizzly bears. On July 15th they started up river again and in ten days reached the three forks which marked the head of the Missouri. Here they camped, while the hunters brought in buffalo, elk and deer. The rest of the party butchered and jerked meat and dressed hides to make shirts, moccasins and leggings for themselves, for by now the clothes they had worn were in rags. The mosquitoes were so bad that the men had to sit in the smoke of the fires to get relief.

This was the place where Sacagawea had been captured, and she now recognized the country. On August 11th they met their first western Indians, a camp of Shoshones. With the help of Sacagawea they made the Indians understand that they wanted to be friends and gave them presents so that the redskins would sell them horses to take them over the continental divide, which lay ahead. To the west they could see lofty

ranges, whose snow-clad peaks shimmered in the sunshine.

On September 2nd, having bought twenty-nine horses from the Shoshones, they hid their canoes, made packsaddles out of the boat oars, loaded the baggage on the horses and started across the mountains. By the 13th they reached Lolo Pass, having met a party of friendly Flathead Indians who sold them eleven more horses. It had been a week of very hard going, along dizzy precipices where a slip meant death. Several packhorses fell and were dashed to pieces, but the party finally emerged safely from the mountains and reached the Lochsa River, on the western slope of the Rockies. They camped on Lolo Creek and called the place "Travelers' Rest."

There was no game in this high country and they soon finished all the jerky they had brought and were reduced to eating their horses, coyotes and even crows. Then they met some friendly Nez Percé Indians, whose name, "pierced noses," came from their habit of hanging ornaments from holes pierced in their noses. These Indians, because of the lack of game in the Columbia River valley, ate mostly fish and the dried roots of the camas and other plants. Lewis bought some camas flour and dried salmon from them, and while it stopped his men's hunger they were all sick from this new diet.

When their pack train reached the forks of the Clearwater River, from which point boats could reach the coast, they camped and began felling large trees to make dugout canoes. This was done by roughly shaping a bow and stern with their axes and then hollowing out the log by burning out the inside and adzing it smooth. When the canoes were finished the men branded their horses so they could recognize them again and left them with friendly Indians until they returned. They buried their packsaddles and a supply of powder to keep them from being stolen and marked the spot carefully so they could find them on the way back.

On October 5th they started down the Snake River, through rushing rapids and white water, where several of the canoes were overturned, forcing the party to stop and dry out the stores. On the 16th they floated out of the Snake into the great Columbia, the first white men to see its reaches east of the Cascade Mountains.

All along the Columbia they saw many Indian villages; the shores were lined with fish weirs, nets and drying racks, for the Flatheads depended for their whole year's food supply on the great run of salmon which came up the river each spring to spawn. The Flatheads were so named because of their custom of compressing the soft skulls of the papooses between two boards until they were flattened at the top.

Lewis and Clark found that there was neither game nor firewood along the riverbanks. They had to buy wood from the Indians and because of the scarcity they learned to eat dogs which the redskins raised for food. Since the Indians had no cooking pots they boiled their meat by putting heated stones in the water in a leakproof basket until the water boiled.

On October 24th the expedition reached the great falls of the Columbia. Mile after mile of treacherous rock-strewn rapids lay before them. They should have portaged around many of the bad places, but winter was approaching and they had to hurry. When they reached a dangerous spot the baggage was carried around. The empty canoes, manned by several good swimmers, shot the rapids. By November 2nd they had survived the great falls and then the Cascades (now buried beneath the deep water behind Bonneville Dam). They had reached tidewater at last.

From now on they encountered constant storms and rain squalls. They were always wet through and often had trouble finding enough level ground along the debris-strewn banks to make camp at night. Food and water were very scarce and swarms of insects constantly plagued them. By now the river had widened into a broad bay and the fierce winds churned up such enormous waves that for days they dared not launch their canoes. Even on good days the water was so rough that many of the men were seasick. The boatmen had to be always on the alert against giant 200-foot floating trees, tossed by the waves so that they became enormous battering rams which could have crushed a canoe like an eggshell.

On December 7th the party crossed the river and

paddled up a creek to a wooded height where they built a winter camp which they called Fort Clatsop, after a local tribe. The Clatsops and the Chinooks, who also lived here, constantly visited the camp during the winter trading fish and roots and stealing anything they could lift.

Fort Clatsop was enclosed by a log stockade 50 feet square, and contained two rows of cabins, one of three and one of four buildings, separated by a parade ground 20 feet wide. It was finished on New Year's Day, 1806, and the men celebrated with a couple of volleys from their rifles. Near the fort stood a large tree, famous for many years for the inscription carved on it which read: *Wm. Clark, Dec. 3, 1805. By land from U.S. in 1804–5.*

After the fort was completed a small camp was set up on the coast. Here relays of men boiled seawater to make salt, which they were in great need of. Hunters went out every day to shoot elk which were in great numbers in the woods. At the fort the meat was dried and the hides cured to make clothes, but much of it spoiled because of the constant rain. Boiled elk and roots was the daily diet, except when Indians brought in fish and fat dogs. Once some Clatsops brought them some hunks of blubber from a stranded whale, which made a welcome change to the table.

Lewis and Clark anxiously scanned the horizon for a ship; the Indians told them that a number of trading vessels put in every year. From a ship they could hope to replenish their vanishing stock of trade goods which would be needed to buy horses and food from the Indians on the way back. They never saw a single ship during their winter on the coast and for some reason President Jefferson failed to send a supply ship. The lack of trade goods was serious. On the way home Captain Lewis had to trade his own uniform coat and hat, his sword and several guns, as well as powder and shot and several badly needed kettles.

The two captains spent much of the winter writing up their journals and working on the maps they had drawn. They also listed all the animals they had seen. Domestic animals were dogs, mules and horses, the latter all descendants of strays brought to the new world by the Spanish Conquistadores. Among the wild beasts were grizzly, brown and black bears, deer, elk, antelope, mountain sheep, wolves and coyotes. They also saw panther, lynx, beaver, foxes, badger, fisher, otter, mink, seal, raccoon, squirrel, rabbits, prairie dogs, skunks, moles, sea lions and chipmunks.

The captains at last gave up hope of meeting a ship; they had to start back soon if they hoped to reach the upper Missouri before next fall's freeze. On April 6, 1806, they loaded their canoes and headed upstream. When they reached the mountains they found that the drifts were too deep and so they waited for five weeks for the snow to melt. At last, on June 14th, they followed the trails the Indians had used for countless years on their way to hunt the buffalo on the plains.

They passed peaks still deep in snow and reached their old camp at Travelers' Rest on June 30th. Here the expedition split.

Lewis's party crossed the divide by a shorter route, to the great falls of the Missouri, in a search for a river which would reach into Canada. He followed the Marias River north for a few miles, but soon saw it was not going in the right direction, and so doubled back to the Missouri.

Clark's party took the old route to the headwaters of the Missouri, where some of his men uncovered the cached canoes and paddled down river. Clark and the rest went overland to the Yellowstone River and followed it down to its mouth where he expected to join Lewis and his men with the canoes.

On the way, Clark was accidentally shot through the thighs by Cruzette while they were hunting elk. The wound was painful but not serious, and Clark dressed it himself and went on. The next day they overtook Lewis and on the same day came upon the camp of two white trappers from Illinois. They were the first white men the explorers had seen for well over a year.

Now the adventure was drawing to a close. On September 23, 1806, they floated out of the Missouri into the Mississippi, and by noon had landed at St. Louis.

The two brave and skillful co-captains had led a party of twenty-nine men, a woman and a baby twice across the continent through thousands of miles of wilderness never before seen by a white man, over several wild, snow-capped mountain ranges, through the hunting grounds of many fierce Indian tribes. In spite of the perils and hardships of the trip they lost only one man, who died of a burst appendix. They had made friends with the Indians and made allies of some, mapped thousands of miles of trackless country and described the geography, animals, birds and topography of mysterious Louisiana. The fur trappers and later the pioneers followed in their footsteps to open up the West.

6. Zebulon Pike

WHILE Lewis and Clark were still on the Missouri far to the westward, young Lieutenant Zebulon Pike was ordered by General Wilkinson, commanding in Louisiana, to explore the upper Mississippi.

At Little Falls, Pike built a small log fort and left his boats there, because they could navigate no farther north. He pressed on with a small party on foot through the snow and ice of a severe midwestern winter. Bad weather prevented him from finding the source of the Mississippi, but he brought back accurate maps of the country he had passed through when he returned to St. Louis in 1806. On the way be reported seeing such vast flights of wild passenger pigeons that they darkened the sky. His hunters killed 298 pigeons in 15 minutes.

In the summer of 1806 Pike was sent to find out more about the border between western Louisiana and Spanish Mexico, which had never been mapped. He was also to try to bring peace between the Kansas and Osage Indians and to explore the upper reaches of the Arkansas and Red rivers.

In October his party of two officers, one doctor, eighteen soldiers, one interpreter, three Osage Indians and a squaw pushed their way through unexplored country filled with hostile Indians, territory which is now Arkansas, Oklahoma, Kansas and Colorado. They traveled as far as the present site of Leadville, Colorado. On the way they examined a towering, snow-capped peak and named it Pikes Peak.

Winter caught the expedition deep among the mountains, but on January 30, 1807, they reached the headwaters of the Rio Grande and followed it south into Spanish territory. In February, Pike was taken prisoner by a squadron of Spanish cavalry and escorted to Santa Fé, where all his papers and maps were confiscated. However, he was well treated by the Spaniards and that summer returned to the American border and released. Six years later, as a brigadier general, he was killed leading his troops at Toronto, during the War of 1812.

7. The Mountain Men

WHEN Lewis and Clark returned to St. Louis their reports of the vast herds of buffalo, the swarming beaver colonies and the great numbers of otter, mink and other fur-bearers stirred the frontier. Fur companies were organized and went up the Missouri in boats and canoes loaded with traps and supplies to establish base camps on its headwaters and on the Yellowstone.

From these camps small parties of trappers went out to search for beaver colonies and bring back the pelts, which were then baled and shipped back to St. Louis. A beaver pelt was worth from three to five dollars, according to size and condition, delivered at a base camp. The trappers were a new breed, tough and able to withstand incredible hardships. Often hard drinkers and brawlers at the base camp, once in the wilderness they were superb woodsmen and well able to take care of themselves. They had to be, to keep from being tortured and scalped by the Indians. These men came to be known as the mountain men.

The mountain man, who often spent many months alone or with one or two companions in the wilderness, was usually heavily bearded and long-haired. He wore a fringed buckskin hunting shirt, a breechclout like an Indian's, leggings and moccasins of deerskin, and a cap of beaver or otter. His clothes were usually so black with grease and dirt that they looked like black patent leather. Everything he wore, he made himself from animals he trapped and cured. For winter he had a heavy blanket or a buffalo robe which he rolled up in at night. On the trail he rode an Indian pony and led at least one packhorse loaded with a supply of powder and lead and a bullet mold, five or six beaver traps, an ax, an awl, a kettle and a skillet. When he could get them he carried a little flour, salt, sugar, tea and lard, but he lived mostly on whatever meat he could kill and a few roots and berries.

To make camp the mountain man simply unloaded the packhorses, hobbled them so they wouldn't wander away while grazing, and built a fire. After he broiled and ate his venison or buffalo tongue, he rolled up in his robe to sleep. When it rained or snowed he tried to find shelter under a ledge or a thickly needled pine or cedar, otherwise he just got wet. If his route traversed rivers or lakes he traveled in a log canoe which he dug out of a large cottonwood log.

The beaver lived in brush and mud huts they built, or under banks along a stream or lake, with the entrances to their houses underwater. If a stream was too shallow they built dams of sticks and mud to form ponds. Their colonies were easy to find, because of the tree stumps around their homes. They dragged the trees into the pond for food; they lived on the bark.

The trapper waded out at dusk and set his trap underwater on one of the beaver runways, anchoring it by fastening the ring at one end of the chain to a pole rammed into the mud. This was to keep the beaver underwater so it would drown before it could gnaw off its forepaw and escape. At dawn the trapper returned, skinned any trapped beaver on the spot and carried the pelts and the tails (for his dinner) back to camp. Since pelts were thicker and more valuable in late fall and early winter, the trapper spent long hours wading in icy water; many were crippled by rheumatism at an early age.

When they brought their pelts to the base most of the mountain men squandered their money on whiskey and trinkets and soon had just enough left to outfit them for another trapping expedition filled with hardship and constant danger. During their wanderings they were usually the first to discover new passes, rivers and lakes and great unsuspected valleys all through the West, but they seldom kept journals or notes. Their discoveries passed by word of mouth, often not believed, until someone like Pike or Frémont rediscovered them and described them in books.

8. John Colter

JOHN Colter, born around 1770 in Virginia, grew
up to become one of the most celebrated of the
mountain men. He died in his early forties, but dur-

ing only seven years he performed such remarkable deeds of daring and endurance that other mountain men considered him one of the greatest.

We hear of him first in the journals of Lewis and Clark, where he was enlisted as a private in their expedition, on October 15, 1803. He was mentioned as one of three men punished for drunkenness at the start, but later became one of the most trusted expert hunters of the party. When Colter applied for permission to resign on the way home, so that he could go on a trapping trip with the two white hunters they met on the Missouri, Captain Lewis let him go because of his fine record.

The three men spent the winter in the mountains but the trip was not successful, and Colter left and paddled downriver alone. At the mouth of the Platte he came upon the boats of a new fur company called the Rocky Mountain Fur Company, led by a Spaniard, Manuel Lisa. They were bound for the Yellowstone and Big Horn country, and Colter joined them.

The fur brigade made camp where the Big Horn flows into the Yellowstone, in October, 1807, and built a fort called Fort Raymond, which was to be headquarters for trapping parties. Lisa was eager to begin trading for furs with the Indians, so someone had to let the redskins in their winter camps know that the trappers had arrived and were ready to do business.

Colter was selected, and he left camp alone with a 30-pound pack, a blanket and his gun, on a 500-mile trip through the mountains in midwinter. After delivering the message to the Crow villages he headed south to the river called the Stinking Water, because of the sulphur in it. Presently he entered a strange, fearful land, where clouds of sulphur-tainted steam rose from cracks in the rock, boiling mud and bubbling tar pools seethed, and great geysers of boiling water erupted in tall fountains.

When Colter returned and described this weird land, nobody believed him. Everybody laughed and called it "Colter's Hell." Later every word was proven true — Colter had discovered what became Yellowstone National Park.

On another expedition Colter, while out with another man in canoes, saw the shores lined with armed Indians who waved them ashore. Colter was seized and stripped naked, but his companion refused to come ashore. He shot an Indian who had wounded him with an arrow, and in an instant, Colter related, the trapper was filled with as many arrows as a porcupine had quills.

Instead of scalping him, the Indians indicated by signs they wanted him to walk away. Puzzled, he started off but soon heard a war whoop and saw some young braves armed with spears leap forward. Now he understood — he was to be run down and killed for sport. He ran for his life, naked and barefooted, through six miles of cactus-covered field, and outdistanced all but one brave who was gaining. With blood streaming from nose and mouth, Colter suddenly turned and leaped at his surprised pursuer, seized his spear and killed him. Then, with only the brave's blanket and spear, he eluded the other Indians and for seven days made his way back to camp in broiling sun by day and bitter cold by night, with only roots and berries to eat.

Soon after this, he told his companions that he reckoned he had used up his luck and that he had had enough narrow escapes from the Blackfeet to last him the rest of his life. He was through, and was leaving the wilderness. This daring, reckless mountain man finally died in bed of jaundice, in November, 1813.

9. Jedediah Smith

JEDEDIAH SMITH, a New Englander born in 1798, moved west with his family. Later he joined General Ashley's Rocky Mountain Fur Company, and became its greatest scout and explorer. He crossed the

Rockies and first explored the country lying between the western slopes and the Great Salt Lake.

On an expedition in 1826, he ranged through the unknown wilds of Utah and eastern Nevada, and pushed to the Colorado River. With fifteen men he spent three tortured, thirsty weeks, crossing the blazing Mojave Desert, then struck the old Spanish Santa Fe–Los Angeles trail and reached the San Gabriel Mission in California. He was ordered to leave by the suspicious Mexicans and so headed north into the San Joaquin valley where the party spent the winter trapping. In the spring Smith and two other men, with seven horses and two pack mules, crossed the snow-filled Sierras after a desperate eight-day struggle. They reached Salt Lake after traversing the entire state of Nevada, a waterless desert. Of their nine animals, one feeble horse and a mule survived. They had eaten the others as they gave out.

Jedediah Smith was killed by Comanches on the Santa Fe Trail when he was only thirty-two, but into his short life he crammed an enormous amount of adventure and danger. He was the first white man to cross the Sierras and the Great Salt Desert. He discovered the famous South Pass. He first explored the great basin between the Rockies and the Sierras, and was also the first white man to enter California from the east, by way of Great Salt Lake and the Mojave.

10. Pushing Westward

IF you look at the Frontier Map of the United States on the end papers of this book you will see that the frontier line marking the farthest advance of the villages and farms of the pioneers still lay to the east of the Appalachians in 1800. By 1830, so many new land-hungry immigrants from Europe had poured into the promised land that the new frontier had reached the Mississippi. Between 1763 and 1800 the population of the young United States had grown from 1,600,000 to 5,300,000.

As the white settlers pushed westward the Indians were driven from their ancient hunting grounds, which was the cause of constant trouble. The War Department built a chain of forts along the frontier and stationed troops in them to try to keep the peace, from Fort Smith in Arkansas to Fort Snelling in Minnesota. Congress realized how badly the Indians had been treated, and so in 1830 decided to give them a permanent home, where they could remain forever. A boundary was drawn, running roughly along the western borders of Wisconsin, Illinois, Missouri, Arkansas and Louisiana, west of which no hunting, trapping or farming by whites would ever be permitted. In 1830 the lawmakers couldn't imagine that white men would ever want to move into this far-off wilderness. This line was no more able to keep back the flood of emigrants than that Proclamation Line of 1763 had been. By 1841, a little over ten years later, the government had stopped trying to keep back the pioneers. Long trains of emigrant wagons began pushing ever westward, especially along the Oregon Trail through Nebraska, Wyoming and Idaho, over the route opened up by

Lewis and Clark. Other settlers went up the Mississippi, the Missouri, the Platte and the Arkansas rivers by bullboat, keelboat and the newly invented river steamers. Still farther west the mountain men, braving the danger of scalping by redskins, ranged far and wide among the wild canyons and rugged passes of the Rockies.

South of the Oregon Trail was a vast, unexplored area, reaching southward to the Mexican outposts in Arizona, New Mexico and Texas, and westward into the basin between the Rockies and the Sierras, which sealed off the California coast, also held by Mexico. The old Spanish Trail running from San Diego across Southern California, Nevada and Utah and curving southeastward through Colorado and New Mexico to the old Spanish capital at Santa Fe, was the only road through this wilderness, and that only through the southern part.

The government at Washington wanted to know more about this great unexplored area, whether there was water and good soil, the direction of the rivers and their navigability, the height of the mountains and the location of passes where wagons might cross. There was still hope that a river which flowed through the mountain ranges to the Pacific might be found.

11. John Charles Frémont

A YOUNG man named John Charles Frémont, born in 1813, son of a French refugee father and a Virginia mother, at the age of twenty-five started an exploring career in the west. In sixteen years, from 1838 to 1954, he was to make more and longer exploring trips, mapping and taking notes of the western country, than any other man of his time.

He had explored the upper Mississippi as assistant to Joseph Nicollet between 1838 and 1841. In 1842 he was commissioned by the government to lead a party, with the famous frontiersman Kit Carson as guide, up the Oregon Trail to Fort Laramie.

By the spring of 1843 he was ready for what was to be the greatest exploring expedition since Lewis and Clark reached the Columbia in 1805. On the 29th of May, Frémont's party of thirty-nine Creoles, French Canadians, and Americans set out from the Missouri River, under the guidance of Thomas Fitzpatrick. This famous scout was a striking man whose hair had turned white in one night during a fearful Indian attack.

The party was armed with Hall's carbines and a 12-pounder brass howitzer on a wheeled carriage which Frémont borrowed from the army. The supplies were carried in twelve carts pulled by mules, and a small spring wagon carried the telescopes, transits and other scientific instruments.

At first Frémont followed the Oregon Trail, then went up the Kansas and Republican rivers, heading for St. Vrain's fort, an emigrant trading post in northeastern Colorado. At the fort they were welcomed and feasted, but most of the post's provisions had been sold to emigrants. All that was left for Frémont's party was a little flour and some powder and ball.

They pushed on into the mountains, finding rough

going for wagons, and reached the South Pass, at an elevation of 7,490 feet, on August 13th. Next they crossed the Green River which flows into the Colorado, a river of wild rapids and deep gorges, emptying into the Gulf of California. They were told by the natives of hidden valleys along the Colorado, almost completely hemmed in by beetling cliffs, valleys filled with great colonies of beaver, which the Indians also used as hiding places for their flocks when pursued by the Spaniards.

Here they were joined by Kit Carson, the famous guide. After crossing very rough country they camped in a cottonwood grove with good grass. Because he had heard that game was very scarce in the high country ahead, Frémont decided to hunt buffalo and dry the meat for later use. Suddenly a horse guard let out a yell and began driving the herd pell-mell into camp. Behind him a band of seventy mounted warriors came screeching over the hilltop brandishing their bows and spears. The horse herd reached the camp safely and now the Indians faced a line of determined, well-armed men, plus a brass cannon loaded with grapeshot.

The Cheyenne war party jerked their ponies to a halt and made peace signs, so Frémont gave them food and tobacco and watched them carefully until they departed at sunset.

On August 21st the expedition reached the Bear River, which flows into the famous Great Salt Lake. Since the lake has no outlet, Frémont had heard strange

73

tales of where the water went. The mountain men believed that a great deadly whirlpool in the center of the lake sucked the water into an underground channel which led to the sea. Actually evaporation takes care of the surplus water, leaving more and more salt in the lake.

All along the Bear River they saw caravans of emigrants, men, women and children living in canvas-covered wagons pulled by oxen. Boys guarded the horses and milk cows, while cooking fires lighted up the riverbanks at night. This was the main emigrant route to Oregon. How different this was from the expedition of Lewis and Clark, who did not see a single white man from the time they left the Mandan camps until they were almost back at St. Louis.

Presently they came to a camp of Shoshone Indians

where they were greeted by a mass of charging horse-men armed with guns, lances and bows, the braves wearing long red-streamered war bonnets reaching to the ground. The Shoshones were friendly though, and invited the whites to their village, where Frémont bought eight horses from them with blankets, red and blue cloth, beads, knives and tobacco. The Indians gave them edible berries, roots and seeds, which the men enjoyed as a change from their meat diet.

Frémont noticed that buffalo were becoming very scarce in this region in this year of 1843. Between 1824 and 1836, travelers had reported that on the trail be-tween the Rockies and the Missouri they were never out of sight of vast herds of buffalo. Because of the slaughter both by Indians and whites the buffalo were rapidly disappearing. Ninety thousand buffalo robes

were being shipped east every summer, and at least twice that many animals were slaughtered just for the marrowbones and tongues for food.

Frémont and five of his men put together a collapsible rubber boat and prepared to navigate Great Salt Lake, probably the first white men to float on the salty, buoyant water. The shores were covered by thousands of waterfowl — geese, ducks and wild swans. The explorers paddled out to visit several barren islands but the wind increased and soon the waves rose so high they had to land beyond their camp to keep from capsizing. One of the party walked back to camp and brought horses to carry their baggage back. Frémont's reports on the valley had much to do with Brigham Young's decision to locate his Mormon colony there four years later.

Now they crossed to the western slopes of the mountains. The road was very rough here, with steep ravines and rocky ridges — hard going for the carts. Now they began to meet the western Indians, who lived mostly on salmon. Each spring when the Pacific salmon swam up the rivers from the coast to spawn, the Indians caught them with nets, weirs and gigs (barbed spears). Braves, squaws and even the children all worked desperately to catch enough salmon and dry them on raised platforms to last until the next spring. There was almost no game available, so besides the fish there were only a few roots and plants to eat. The Indians were miserably poor and almost naked because there

WASHINGTON MONTANA NORTH DAKOTA MINNESOTA

Nez Percé *Blackfeet*

Chinooks *Mandans*

OREGON IDAHO SOUTH DAKOTA

Walla Walla *Snakes* *Sioux*

WYOMING IOWA

CALIFORNIA NEVADA *Shoshones* *Crows* NEBRASKA

UTAH *Cheyennes* *Omahas* *Iowas* MISSOURI

IOWA

COLORADO KANSAS

Kansas

CLAIMED BY SPANISH

ARIZONA NEW MEXICO OKLAHOMA ARKANSAS

☐ Louisiana Purchase

▬▬ Lewis and Clark Expedition 1804

▬ ▬ Frémont Expedition 1843

were no animals to supply skins or furs. Often in winter they were so starved that some of them became cannibals.

On October 20th Frémont's men saw for the first time the mighty Columbia and found that traders' boats came up the river this far from salt water. Here they camped and while most of the party repaired gear and made packsaddles, Frémont and three of the men bought a canoe from the Indians and headed downriver for Vancouver where they hoped to buy supplies. On the river they passed many large arklike rafts built by emigrants to carry their wagons and goods down the stream to the fertile valleys of western Oregon.

Frémont portaged around the same Cascades whose roar Lewis and Clark had heard forty years before and presently reached the Hudson's Bay Company post at Fort Vancouver. The post was supplied by ships from England. At anchor in the river lay the bark *Columbia,* about to sail for London as soon as the bateaux bringing overland mail from Hudson Bay and western Canada arrived.

Frémont was able to buy food, ammunition and supplies, and arranged for a Mackinaw boat and some canoes, manned by Canadian and Indian boatmen, to take them upstream to his camp. He would have liked to paddle down to the mouth of the Columbia to see the Pacific, but the fogs and howling gales of the rainy season made it impossible.

Frémont started south on November 25th; the party

was twenty-five strong, with 104 horses and mules to carry the baggage. They had flour, dried peas and tallow for cooking and they drove a herd of California cattle for beef. Because of the wild country ahead they abandoned their little instrument wagon; now the only wheels were those of the little brass howitzer. There was already ice on the streams as they began their daring winter hike through the high mountains.

They passed through the region of the Klamath Lakes, struggling through rough country deep in snow. Their constant concern was to find grass for the animals, since they couldn't carry enough hay or oats to feed them. Without grazing the pack animals soon grew too weak to carry a load, and the weaker ones were butchered and eaten.

For some time Frémont had been trying to head east to try to cross the mountains and reach Fort Hall for provisions, but at last he was convinced that the solid wall of mountains in that direction was impassable. He headed south through western Nevada where the going was easier.

On January 29th the expedition crossed a high pass and camped where the wind had blown the snow off the grass so the animals could graze. Here they saw Indians on snowshoes, skimming over the drifts like birds. They brought in pine nuts to trade, and the men found that when the nuts were roasted they were very good.

Now before them was a region of very rugged ranges

where the snow was so deep that the Indians told them they could never get through in winter. Frémont resolved to try anyhow, with an advance party on horseback to break trail, but they had to abandon their little cannon at last. On February 2nd, with an Indian guide, they began crossing the Sierras at an elevation of 6,760 feet. The snow was so deep the horses couldn't struggle through the drifts. They camped that night in a grove of pines in the open. A huge fire was built, pine boughs were cut on which to spread their blankets out of the

snow, and they went to sleep in bright moonlight, with
the temperature 10 degrees above zero.

Next morning they found that their guide had deserted, so Frémont set the men to making snowshoes
for themselves and sledges for the baggage, while he
and a small party went ahead to break trail and explore. When they had climbed the next peak they saw
spread before them the valley of the Sacramento, bor-
dered by a line of low mountains Kit Carson recognized as the coastal range.

They emerged from the mountains on March 6, 1844, and reached Sutter's Fort on the American River, just above where it joined the Sacramento. John Sutter was a Swiss who had received a land grant from the Mexicans. He had built a prosperous settlement, raised crops and started a sawmill. His fort was a square adobe structure, mounting twelve pieces of artillery, big enough for a garrison of 1,200, although he had only a company of forty uniformed Indians. A few years later, in 1849, the discovery of gold at his sawmill would bring such a rush of gold seekers that his crops were overrun and Sutter himself ruined.

Frémont's party arrived in bad shape; out of 104 horses and mules they had started with from the Columbia only 33 reached Sutter's. Sutter obligingly sold the explorers what they needed, and on March 24th Frémont resumed the journey, with 130 horses and mules, 25 beef cattle and five milk cows. The party still wanted to turn east, but had to march 500 miles to the south before they could find a pass through the solid wall of the Sierra Nevada.

At last they found a pass at the head of the San Joaquin River and began making their way through pleasant oak groves amid fields brilliant with golden poppies and blue lupines. Game was again plentiful, herds of elk, antelope and wild horses grazed in the meadows, and they saw many grizzly bears. On the trail they met an Indian from the Spanish missions who told Frémont not to go directly east to Salt Lake after he crossed the mountains. Beyond the mountains, the Indian said, was a burning desert without water or grass. He advised following the old Spanish Trail leading to Santa Fe.

Even on the Spanish Trail they suffered from thirst, and they had several brushes with hostile Indians who tried to steal their horses. The hostiles killed one of the men with an arrow. On May 16th they left the trail on which they had traveled 440 miles in 27 days and camped in a fresh green meadow with clear cold springs at a place called in Spanish Las Vegas. On the 23rd they crossed the Sevier River on rafts made by tying bundles of rushes together. Here they lost one man, when the hammer of his gun caught as he pulled it toward him, and sent a bullet through his head.

At last, on May 24, 1844, they reached Great Salt Lake, which they had left the September before. They had made a great circle of 3,500 miles, explored the great ranges of the Rockies and the Sierras, measuring the peaks and mapping the area thoroughly. Frémont proved that the Columbia was the only river which pierced the Coast Range to reach the Pacific. He proved that the Buenaventura and other rivers which were shown on many maps as crossing the Sierras to the sea were only imaginary. He proved that there could never be a water crossing from the Great Plains to the Pacific, because the Rockies to the east and the Sierras to the west hemmed in a great basin over 400 miles wide into which all the streams flowed.

Altogether, Frémont made five western expeditions, the last one in 1853, during which he crossed and re-crossed the continent from the Columbia to the Mexican border. His journals and observations encouraged the pioneers to emigrate to the West.

12. The Westward Tide

THE 1850's saw the close of the great drama of American exploration. Frémont and Kit Carson, and before them Lewis and Clark, Zebulon Pike, and the mountain men of Ashley's Rocky Mountain Fur Company, John Colter, Jedediah Smith and Jim Bridger, had unlocked the secrets of the Far West. These men had followed the great rivers which flowed into the Mississippi to their headwaters in the mountains in search of that four-legged gold mine, the beaver. They had straggled through the high passes and explored the Great Basin. Some had reached the Pacific far to the north by floating down the Columbia. Others had crossed the Sierras and reached the fertile valleys of coastal California. Still others struggled through the parched, blazing desert country of the Southwest.

Long trains of emigrant wagons followed in their footsteps. In the Southwest, first the Texans in 1836, and then the Californians in 1846 freed themselves from Mexican rule. A year later, victory in the Mexican War brought the rest of the southwest under the Stars and Stripes.

In 1849 the discovery of gold at Sutter's Mill brought a new onrush of people to fill the great empty West. By the end of the Civil War only one kind of exploring remained to be done — a search for the best routes for the new transcontinental railroads, which would soon tie together the edges of the continent with each other by steel rails.

By the beginning of the twentieth century vast herds of cattle and flocks of sheep grazed on the Great Plains where once the buffalo had been king, and miles of golden, waving wheat covered the onetime prairie-dog villages. From the Atlantic to the Pacific the great nation had been mapped and surveyed and peopled, all under one flag, in a span of 200 years. Each wave of emigration was always led by a few brave, hardy Americans who explored the unknown ahead and brought back the word.

GLOSSARY

GLOSSARY

BADGER — A burrowing mammal with short, thick legs, and and long claws on the forefeet.

BALE — A large bundle of goods, usually tightly bound and wrapped.

BAROMETER — An instrument for determining atmospheric pressure and for judging probable changes of weather.

BASIN — A tract of country drained by a river and its tributaries.

BOTANY — The science of plants.

BOW — The forward part of a ship.

BREASTWORK — A defensive fort of moderate height, usually one hastily thrown up.

CELESTIAL NAVIGATION — Plotting a course by using the stars as points of reference.

CHRONOMETER — A highly accurate instrument for measuring time.

FLINTLOCK — An old-fashioned gun or pistol lock having a flint in the hammer for striking a spark to ignite the charge.

FORECASTLE — The upper deck in the forward part of a ship.

FRONTIER — The border or advance region of settlement and civilization.

GARRISON — A fortified place where troops are quartered.

GAUNTLET — An Indian-style military punishment where the offender must run between two files of men who strike him with clubs, etc., as he passes.

GEOLOGY — The science of studying the history of the earth and its life; especially as recorded in the rocks.

HOWITZER — A short light cannon.

KEELBOAT — A shallow, covered freight boat with timbers extending along the center of the bottom of a ship, but no sails.

LAND GRANT — A grant of land by the government.

MACKINAW BOAT — A flat-bottomed boat, used especially on the upper Great Lakes and their tributaries.

PALISADE — A long pointed stake, set with others in a close row as a defense.

PAPOOSE — A young child of North American Indian parents.

PELT — A skin of a fur-bearing animal.

PIROGUE — A dugout canoe.

PORTAGE — A carrying of boats, goods, etc., overland between navigable waters; also, the route over which they are carried.

POWDER HORN — A container for gunpowder.

PROCLAMATION LINE — A boundary line established by statute in 1673 along the eastern slopes of the Appalachians from Quebec to Florida west of which no white men could settle or hunt.

SEXTANT — A navigational instrument used to observe altitude in order to determine latitude and longitude.

STERN — The back end of a ship.

WAIST — The center part of a ship.

WEIRS — Stakes set in a stream for taking fish.

ZOOLOGY — A science of studying the animal kingdom and its members.

INDEX

The Author

WALTER BUEHR has long been a favorite author-illustrator of young people who enjoy the color and romance of history. He has written and illustrated books on the Crusades, *The Crusaders*, the era of the feudal castle, *Knights and Castles and Feudal Life* and *Chivalry and the Mailed Knight*, and the explorations of the Americas, *The French Explorers in America* and *The Spanish Conquistadores in North America*. His impressive list also includes books about communications and the different carriers of commerce and industry. Mr. Buehr, himself a sailing man, has never lived far from the sea. He and his wife Camilla, a fashion illustrator, live in Noroton, Connecticut. A short distance from their home you will find, of course, a moored sailboat.